Morning Will Surely Come

Poems of the Black African Struggle

Series Two

Ikechi Akurunwa

i

Books by Ikechi Akurunwa

Poetry

In the Palm of Her hand
You Grew Taller Than the Palm
Morning Will Surely Come

Non-Fiction

The Cardinal Laws of Freedom
Self-Examination: The Path to Being Free & Staying Free

BOOK EXPRESS PUBLISHING HOUSE books may be ordered through booksellers or www.goexpresspublishing.com

ISBN: 978-0-9729525-1-4 (Paperback)
ISBN: 978-1-955495-01-1 (Hardback)
ISBN: 978-0-9729525-5-2 (ebook)

First Printing
Printed in the United States of America
Print information available on the last page.
Library of Congress Control Number: 2021935976 (Paperback)
Library of Congress Control Number: 2021937718 (Hardback)

BOOK EXPRESS PUBLISHING HOUSE
Atlanta, Georgia
www.goexpressbulishing.com

DEDICATION

To every African
dreaming of a free Africa.

Contents

PROLOGUE

Morning Will Surely Come is intended to tell the story of Africa from a poetic viewpoint. Its focus is not on any individual African or country; instead, it draws the curtain of the African dawn for the reader to see the face of Africans forging through the wild winds of colonialism, tyranny, and self-inflicted injuries. It unveils the face of the African struggle, those who are clawed to death in the journey, and those who claw through the dark to rise to the top.

Morning Will Surely Come is not only the story of Black Africa. It's a book that tells the story of Africa's successes and failures, as well as the callousness of the West. The cost of hiding the wounds, the scars, and the dirty laundry of Africa is too high; so is the price Africans are paying for Europe's continued exploitation. Today, I lament with the voice of poetry.

Ikechi Akurunwa

Morning Will Surely Come

ONE

Africa, to watch you burn daily
and not try to save you
is a sin I cannot bear.

Ikechi Akurunwa

Invasion

If this wild wind whirling
stirring up
storms of dust around our houses
was only a passing wind,
why did it linger until its plume
turned our sky dark?

After a new hand emerged from the West
bearing the dark shroud of deception
to cover the eyes of questioning Africans,
our land began to die from asphyxiation.

Can't you see how the claws
of the growing hand
are ripping up our harbors, villages and cities,
and uprooting our ancient roots like weeds?

Can't you see how this crooked hand
has brought down the thrones
of Africa's great leaders and lifted high
the thrones of Africa's worst leaders,
to the great delight of the West?

Can't you see how its large nostrils
trail the faintest scent of our wealth

like a bloodhound trailing blood?

Can't you see how it hovers
over our skies like a hungry hawk
until it snatches from our land,
the last of our surviving chicks.

You doubting Thomas!
Can't you see that since England
and France and Portugal
came to Africa with this eerie wind
of suppression and exploitation,
their cheeks and chins
have been growing fatter and fatter,
while Africa's starved and abused flesh
has been growing thinner and thinner?

Soon, my friend, soon,
their growing addiction
to the treasures of Africa
will make Africans the world's
most vulnerable endangered species.

How Far They Can Go

Though they saw the tremors
from their iron feet smother
all the roses in our land,
they still trailed the wind
that carried the fragrance
of the last rose
to our nostrils,
to make sure we wallowed
in our dreary world,
from day to day,
without the soothing smell of a rose.

All through the years
they watched our forests slowly
wither from the famine
they imposed with colonialism,
yet, day after day,
they combed our land
for any surviving tree
to make sure they denied us
the joy of seeing another emerald eye
burn in our sky
from the stamens
of our towering trees.

Year after year, they have stood
at the door of our treasury,
starved our children
until many developed marasmus,
yet, they wonder why our children
are dying or fleeing our land.

They saw our farmlands
turned into wastelands
from the oil spilled by their rigs,
yet, they have not surrendered an inch
of the poisoned lands and seas
to starving African farmers and fishermen.

It's obvious Africa is the honeycomb
Europe wants to milk dry,
but there might be more to this craving,
more than our eyes can see.

Perhaps, it's more than greed.
Perhaps, it's more than gluttony.
Perhaps, it's a disease,
a disease nothing can cure.

Labels

Maybe, the reason Europe,
for many centuries,
has been screaming,
"black, black, black"
in the face of Africans
is because she has something to hide.

Or maybe, it's a way
to distract our eyes
from her concealed snares,
from her constantly
discharging guns,
from the shadows of her dark ships
disappearing into the night
with our looted treasures?

Or maybe, it's a way to avoid
explaining to the world
why her hands are firmly stuck
in Africa's cookie jar?

If Africa is indeed a dark continent,
then what is the West still doing
in Africa for over four centuries?
Why is Europe still swimming

in Africa's fragrant rivers,
tainting them with greed?

Why has England refused
to release her claws
from the bleeding flesh of Africa?
Why has France refused
to retract their canines sunk
into the jugular of Africa?

By screaming, "black, black, black"
every day, Europe has taught
the world the magic word
to disarm Africa.
She has made Africa
to look as she wants it,
a continent caught in the middle
of the letters of a nickname
coined to steal her glory.

When will Europe admit to the world
that the reason her heart still beats
is because of Africa's wealth
daily siphoned to feed her crookedly
greed-bent mouth?

When?

Unanswered Questions

Ask my heart how to leap out of my chest
at the crackle of a sneaky thunder
and you will have a ready answer.

Ask my eyes how to make rain
when poked by a malicious finger
and you will have a ready answer.

Ask my stomach how to growl
when it's tormented by hunger
and you will have a ready answer.

But ask me why the tropical sun
blazes every day with so much anger,
sometimes, surging through the air like wildfire,

or why the African sky is always dark
while the sun is blazing,
and I have no answer for you.

I have no answer why in Africa
ants live in castles, and elephants are left
to squat in little huts until they die.

I have no answer why in Africa, the tortoise

is always carried across the finish line,
to humiliate the greyhound.

I have no answer why tyranny and subjugation
are imposed on Africans every day
like criminals on a life sentence.

Maybe, one day,
the patience of our children
will run out, and they will scream

from their submerged caves,
from their filthy prison walls,
from their barren villages and cities.

They will scream until those European lords
that forced different African tribes together
to form nonviable African countries

to make it easy for them to rule forever,
will be moved to seek solutions
for the problems they created.

Abe's Memories of Hate Crime

For a long time, what we saw
was only the shadow
of a marauding nighthawk
until the night every firefly,
every glow-worm,
every moon and star,
in the dark South African sky,
marshaled out, one after the other,
to expose his face.

But the lights did not sear his sight,
or dull his knives or senses,
or melt the barrels of his guns.
Feeling untouchable in his white skin,
he vowed to take more black lives.
And the more he kept his promise
the more the fear in our hearts grew.

There was nothing human about him;
indeed, no blood flowed in his veins.
His heart was colder than the gravestones
that marked the tombs of his victims.

Like a fly attracted to a naked wound,
the era of Apartheid unchained the beast in him;

the dark era when South African natives

were seen by white invaders as nothing
but bags of trash to be disposed
by any means necessary.

But when he thought
he was just
beginning his killing spree
the wind of justice revved and rattled
the racial flag boldly flying in the air
until it ripped it apart,
bringing Apartheid to an end.

After the strong cord of Apartheid was broken,
power changed hands, and Mandela,
the bona fide son of South Africa,
became president.

And shortly after, the bell of justice
rang loud in the streets of Georgetown
until the serial killer was apprehended
and brought to justice.

And on the faithful day
that he was thrown into jail for life,
the joy was irrepressible in Georgetown.
Black men ran out of their houses in jubilation,
leaping as high as they could into the air,

shouting joyfully, unable to hold back their tears.

And the women of Georgetown
left their food on the stoves to burn
and poured into the streets,
dancing and singing with great joy,
until their throats cracked.

But at night, when the streets died down,
the sinister image of the serial killer
still lingered in their minds
like a bad dream,
like a chapter of their lives
that has not been completely closed.

Lethabo's Remembrance of Apartheid

Like a leech, Apartheid
drained our blood, night and day,
until many were exhausted,
their souls overtaken
by bitterness.

Like the pulley of a deadly device
Apartheid stretched us
until we broke
into a thousand pieces
like raffia ribbons, forcing
some of our greatest warriors
to bow and surrender.

Those were the worst days of South Africa,
days the spirit of hatred
that had invaded our land
tested our resolve and resilience,

days the strangers
that forcefully took our land
shook it violently and mercilessly,
flaunting their guns at us daily
to get us to crawl on our knees
to do their bidding.

And as for those Pharisees,
those smiling and beguiling serpents,
those sermonizing Leviathans
who came in their company
with shining Bibles,
they were Europe's secret warriors.
That was why they kept sealed lips
as many South Africans
were unjustly murdered
with guns and blunt force,
turning their faces away
all the time that the cruel fire of racism
was slowly burning South Africa to ashes.

Their long silence prolonged
the evil days of Apartheid
and made its scars deep and indelible.
They helped light a flame
that burned the innocent alive,
a flame whose embers
will never completely die
in the streets of South Africa,
or in the hearts of the natives.

Fleecing Africa

Is there a mask
that does not have
something to hide?

Is there a weight
heavier
than a false crown?

Is there a poison
deadlier than the one
that slowly kills?

Which mask
is darker
than World Bank,

the mask the world wears
as she fleeces Africa
and other impoverished nations?

Tell me. Which mask
is darker
than World Bank?

Which mask

is so, so, thick with darkness
like Word bank?

Maybe, You Don't Know

Maybe you don't know that Africa
is for sale to the highest bidder?
Or perhaps you don't know that Hague,
with the rest of the West,
have long rendered the verdict
that Africans have no right
to their lives, their dreams,
their lands, and their riches.

And from the day they sentenced
Africa to a life of poverty and misery,
each time Africa takes a step forward
their callous hands tighten the wrench
until Africa takes two steps backward.

Today, the locusts and caterpillars
they hired to hasten the demise of Africa
by first devouring her heavily
leaved and fruitful vines,
claim they have no time or patience
to nibble at the leaves.

They claim they have no time or patience
to wait for the bees to pollinate
the flowers of the blooming trees,

or to wait for the rain
to wash their dusty leaves clean,
or to wait for the landscape
to sow new garments to avoid
the shame of being stripped naked.

They vowed to use their sharp teeth
to shred the leaves so fast the skyline
will have nowhere to hide,
except behind clouds and mountains.

They have vowed to use their sharp claws
to scrupulously strip even the balk of the stems,
rendering the trees so undesirable
no bird would want to dance
or sing on their branches again;
no star or moon would like to lay
their hallowed heads again
on their shoulders.

They have vowed to turn every tree
into an eyesore, leaving each one
wretched and shriveled, so that no wind
can kiss its leafy lips again,
and no fruit will ripen or twinkle like stars
or glow like the sun on her branches.

And the plans of these traitors
to turn Africa into a barren land

with nothing left but the unsightly carcass
of a once flourishing land,
seem to be succeeding.

No one, no one
is opposing them
or standing in their way.
No one, not even those Africans forgotten
in their dry and sinking land,
or left buried in desert sands,
where every thirsty mouth fights
for every drop of sweat that drips
from the hot temple of the sky.

Friend, maybe, you too don't know
that no one is standing in the way
of these zealous plunderers
bleeding Africa to death.

No one, no one
is standing
in their way!

Africa is for sale
to the highest bidder.

Nothing lasts forever

But today, I opened my eyes wide
and I saw some Baobab trees withering.
I witnessed the walls of houses
that were once elegant
shedding teary scales of old paints,
irons bars that once glittered
now rusty and frothy.
I saw fallen thrones,
thrones with dead gods,
dead fountains,
dead clocks and broken bells.

It looked like another country
but it was my country.
It looked like another continent
but it was my continent.

I looked at the world
and it was naked,
revealing the forgotten marks of death
slowly and silently
gnawing away her flesh.

Nothing lasts forever, my friend,
nothing last forever;

not even the pillars that hedge
your thrones and castles,

or the delicious offerings of the praises of men,
or the soothing hands of your mistresses,
or the wild drumbeats of fame and riches,
or the intoxication of power.

Nothing lasts forever, my friend,
nothing lasts forever.
When it's time for the wind
of retribution to blow,
all it will take is one tiny fragment
from the roaring arrow of judgment
for justice to be served.

Nothing lasts forever, my friend,
nothing lasts forever.
When it's time
for judgment, or death,
all it will take
is one missed syllable,

or one stubble,
one stagger,
to end it all.

TWO

Even a wildfire ends its rage,
even a torrential rain ends its siege,
even the night retracts its dark face,
but why is the drumbeat
of subjugation and tyranny in Africa
a never-ending story?

Ikechi Akurunwa

What Else is New?

i

What else is new to Africans
about the West?

Is it the whitewashed crown
they bestowed
upon their African puppets
to make them objects of ridicule
to the world?

Or how Black African countries
have been made
the cheapest commodity
on the Western auction block?

Or how the Western merchants
gather annually at Hague
or London or New York
to bid on the leftovers
of Africa's treasures?

And each time they gather
the glee on their faces
as they force their poisonous pills

down the throats of sleeping African leaders,
reveal to the keen eye
how the West has perfected
the act of deception.

ii

What else is new to Africans
about their leaders?

Is it how some of them
help the West
darken Africa's moon,
leaving us constantly in the dark?

Or how some of them
have become the Bar-Lev line
for corrupt Western
bureaucrats and lords,
giving them free access
to the vaults that house
African treasures?

Or is it how they turn into jellies
at the sound of a few pennies,
becoming easily pliable
in the hands of every brigand
demanding his share

of the African wealth?

iii

What else is new to the world
about Africans?

Maybe it's our sealed lips,
our utter silence—
the utter silence of our grown men,
the utter silence of our grown women,
the utter silence of our elders,
the utter silence of our leaders,
the utter silence of the whole land of Africa,
in the face of overbearing
tyranny and exploitation.

What struck us dumb
on this great vast universe
leaving our continent filled
with the confusing voices
of angry seas battling
with angry waves and winds?

How long
will we be spectators,
a voiceless people,

daily watching the world
harden our lives like stone?

It's Dark There

It's dark there,
beneath the brow of the African dawn
where the bells of slavery and tyranny
are roaring.

It's dark there,
between Europe's trigger finger
and Africa's lifeless thumb
locked in endless ceremonial handshakes.

It's dark there,
between the kissing lips of Western lords
and their African puppets.

It's dark there,
between the bars that imprisoned
the dreams and the future
of our children—

children wheeled dawn
a dark and mocking path
where it is difficult
to thread their dying hope
through the clogged eye
of the African morning.

Look at their faces.
They are scared,
scared as they ride
the turbulent currents of hunger
whirling in their stomachs
like a wild sea.

They are scared,
scared of endless nights of gales
brimming with wrath
and rumbling thunder.

They are scared,
scared of day after day of furious clouds
and the unholy aromas of a defiled land.

They are scared;
our children are scared.
Look at their faces.

Hardened Earth

After being schooled by greed,
our hardnosed leader
hardened our land like a rock
to forcefully bend our will and crush our spirit
until we bow and worship him.

Today, the heart of everyone
has hardened like a rock,
the ground has hardened like a rock,
rivers have hardened like a rock,
carnations have hardened like a rock.

And death, burning with fury,
prowls through the land
with hands and feet hard as a rock.

Somedays, the overwhelming
premonition of doom
and the thick cloud of gloom
hovering over us
like a terrifying darkness,
makes us shiver
and shed dark tears,

tears

hard as a rock.

Troubled Land

Here, on this battered land of Africa,
weevils eat better than children,
weeds grow fatter than women,
grasses grow taller than men,
so tall they nick the edges of my pen
each time I try to uproot them.

Now the throat of my pen is swollen,
so swollen that sometimes
it is gagged by words
too thick for it to regurgitate,
words awakened in my heart
by the sound of terrors in our land.

Oh bandaged land of Africa!
When will your hands be untied
so that you can give our children
the bread and wine they need?

Oh clogged rivers of Africa!
When will your channels be unclogged
so that you can flow and water
our dry and thirsty land?

Oh sanguineous flies!

When will you retract your long proboscis
so that Africa's moribund body can heal?

The Handwriting

i

If the voices of children
are no longer heard
on their playgrounds
when their stomachs are full,

if the laughter of youth
is no longer heard in the streets
when a new fashion is in vogue;

if the songs of mothers
are no longer heard
while they are rocking
their babies to sleep;

if, at any time,
the invisible hands of fear
seal the mouths of our women,
our youth, our children,

or if, at any time,
there is a monotonous
and eerie sound of grief
and anguish in the air,

know that another tyrant,
another traitor,
has ascended the throne.

ii

When all the trees
begin to get stunted,
mid-summer,

when all the birds
stops to sing
in springtime,

when all the rivers dry up
and lands become cracked
and parched in the wet season,

when the tremor from the feet
of an aberrant shadow reverberates
until old scars begin to bleed,

when the bells of dreams
fall silent like the sealed lips
of the dead,

when the air is thick
with threats and the voices

of violence;

when there are senseless killings
and life has little
or no value at all,

know that another tyrant,
another traitor,
has risen to power.

The Sound of Pain

Africans know the sound of pain,
the pain of being squeezed
into the narrow crevices
in the palms of the West
to make it easier for them
to break or crush our bones
when necessary.

No day goes by that the call
for freedom by Africans is not met
with the strong wave of suppression
by the West and their African brigands.

There is never a day in Africa
without Africans thrashing
in the cage of captivity, rattling
their heavy chains of bondage
as they are tortured by despots
installed and licensed by Europe
to institutionalize slavery and poverty.

All over Africa, the air is constantly
filled with subjugated voices
begging for food with four hands,
and four mouths and four eyes,

people the soles of their feet
have cracked
from standing for too long in the sun
begging for crumbs,

people whose backs have hunched
from bearing the heavyweight
of poverty for too long,

people whose throats have dried
from endlessly praising every passerby
to pry a few pennies from their hands,

people whose fingers have wrinkled
from holding for too long
their sun-burned begging bowls,

people whose lives
have been unjustly caught
in the callous jaws
of perennial exploitation
and subjugation of Africa.

Silent Killers

Every day,
from the hidden window
of a fragile soul,
the unseen eye of an African child
stares through the dark African veil,
looking for someone to lead
their wasting generation
out of the thickening darkness.

For too long, we left every weed
to grow on our land. We neglected
every tiny scratch on the skin of Africa
until it grew into a festering wound,
and now our children are demanding
to know why there are blisters and scars
all over their body.

There is no care, no empathy.
And if we continue
on this path of indifference,
the dark broom in the stiff hands of this era
will keep sweeping fear
into their young hearts
until they fall apart
like a sack that could no longer bear

its heavyweight.

Last night, my eyes were robbed of sleep
by the discordant notes of pride
flying from the lips of a babbler.
I did not hear the voice of all the cancers
growing in the subdued flesh of our government.
I did not hear the footsteps of all the blood cells
forming deadly clots in the veins of our land.
I heard only the noise of a babbler
who wanted the silent and apathetic world
to hear him.

I know the foolishness in pride,
but I will not spend my time
blaming babblers for the problems
of Africa or the world.
I blame those who live and die in silence,
those who see evil and keep their lips sealed,
those who see the tears of hungry children
and turn their greed-laced faces away,
those in whose mouth
truth is murdered every day.

They are the reason,
day after day,
the sun is not seen
rising in the African sky at dawn.
They are the reason the African child

endlessly stares
through the veiled African morning,
looking for any glimmer of hope.

Robbed

Until I grew up and saw dreams bleed
from the veins of living Africans,
I thought dreaming was everyone's right.
But now I know that in Africa
dreams are empty wishes,
fantasies, fairy tales,
the rhetoric of the wind.

Now I know that every day
Africans bear on their backs
the weight of their murdered dreams,
the weight they must drag
through dreamless nights and days
to eke out a living.

That's why at thirty, their veins
have been clogged by pain,
and their souls deeply scarred
by endless battles with wild birds
pecking their wounds,
making them hard to heal.

But despite all the ravages
of tyranny and imperialism,
some still find the courage

to shield their little flickering
light of hope from the wild wind
as they plod through sweltering
nights and days
of oppression and suppression.

Most of them live
with the guilt of failing
in life
as if they were given
any chance to succeed.

Sadly, the guilt
follows them to their graves,
to graves with tombstones
devoid of the stories of their lives,
devoid of the actual cause of their death—
the crushing pain
they silently bore
in their heart
till death.

The truth now hidden
in the grave forever.

Thabisa's Racism Scars

There is too much for me
to tell you in one day
about the sorrows I bear
because of my brown skin.

It's a horror story that makes me,
like an ostrich, sometimes
bury my head in the sand
to silence the voice of doubt,
fear, resentment, and anger
stirred up daily inside my soul.

Sometimes, I weep
like an unwanted child,
like a child who does not know
who to run to or trust.

And the longer the day,
the longer the battle,
the battle I'm constantly
confronted with, whether I am
in Mississippi or Johannesburg.

Yesterday, a kind man offered
to help me carry one

of the grocery bags in my hand,
but he never knew I bore
a heavier weight inside.
He pitied me because of the scars
on my face, but he didn't know
I had deeper scars in my soul,
scars with grooves carved
by the knife of racism,
scars with calcified ledges,
and spasms of unhealed wounds.

It's a burden I bear every day,
in a world of many contradictions,
a world with dark cinematic scenes
in which I am always cast
as the foil character,
the antagonist, the villain,
by those who call me their friends
but don't want me to live
in their neighborhoods,
those who call me their Christian sister
but don't want me in their house-fellowships.

It's a daily ordeal, a systematic
stripping of the dignity
of the black man, so-called;
a systematic suppression
that has become my reality,
the reality of being born an African,

or with brown or black skin,
no matter which part of the world
I decide to live.

And there is more to say,
but I cannot exhaust them in one day.
There is more: the nods and the crackles
of the fireworks in their eyes.
There is more: the flaring
nostrils and the growls.
There is more: the drawn blinds and the blindness.
There is more: the silence, the long silence,
as if you don't exist,
as if you are not visible,
as if you are not human—
the silence, the long silence,
the silent footsteps
that are never heard.

There is more.

The Tears of Luan

Every day, we watch our politicians
kiss the foul mouth of vanity
and defend their futility
with perturbing absurdity,
but we must not say a word.

There is not a day we don't see them
disregarding and disparaging
the laws they made, threatening
to trample with their muddy boot,
anyone who mutters a word against them.

In places where the fragrance
of the rose has died, or on those farms
where every green leaf has mottled,
we still see them fanning the flame
of corruption with their lying tongues,
but we must keep sealed lips.

Even on the holy day of Sunday,
we still see them eating the bread of greed
and defiling every sacred creed,
but we must pretend not have seen
or witnessed their sacrilegious deeds.

So, every day, we are forced
to bury their vile deeds
piously in our souls.

Somedays, the weight is so heavy
that we groan and moan
until the echoes of our throbbing heart
become the only music we hear.

Some nights, the burden is so unbearable
that the nights are worn-out before dawn
by our clattering teeth.

It has become customary
to silently stare silently at evil,
evil so loud
no one with a conscience
can breadth
or sleep in its presence.

There, amid utter darkness, we exist.
There, amid great evil we live,
day after day,

our flesh begging
for redemption or death.

Ikechi Akurunwa

THREE

I bear the same wound
other Africans are nursing.
That's why their pain and anguish
have become my burden.

For Their Sake

The entire army of White Bellbirds
and Screaming Pihas
have been at war with my ears,
even when they know
I have no room in my head
to entertain their howling contest.

I have lent my ears
to the pain of other Africans.
That's why even when I stand
in a lonely African street,
I still hear their voices
reverberating like thunder,
voices of suppressed pain,
voices of sorrows trapped
in bleeding hearts.

In each solitary room,
in each solitary hour,
unspoken words die
in the mouth of the poor,
and grief burns
like acid in the hearts
of those whose voices
may never be heard,

those that quietly die
in their misery.

For their sake,
I will not be distracted
by the yelling White Bellbirds and Pihas
as I write their stories,
the stories
of the forgotten people of Africa,

people who, no matter
how many times they cry,
no one sees their tears.
No matter how many times
they pass through the fire,
no one comes to their rescue.
But when they die, people gather
to give loud and long eulogies.

For their sake,
today, I engrave this poem
on the palms of my hands.

The Price

And so, for many years
we bottled up our anger,
our frustrations,
our vengeful desires
and bitter venoms,
deep in our souls,
like a maltreated orphan.

From year to year
we accepted our fate,
enduring the evil machinations
of a rabblerousing king
incensed with being feared
like thunder.

We were so good at hiding our pain
that no matter how many times
the tyrant looked at our faces,
he could not see the rage
seething inside our hearts.

We turned our hearts into a chamber
where we imprisoned
our anger and feelings,
a makeshift clinic

where we bandaged our wounds.

We lived every day making sure
that from his throne he would not see
our bodies withering
like a rose left in the hot sun,
so that our death would not gladden
his dark heart.

We bottled up our pain and anger
until the day the brook
of our patience dried up,
the day our trembling hands
got tired of stroking his fragile ego.

Immediately, he grew bitter
like an angry river,
and nothing we did pleased him anymore.

Even our rooftops became too rusty
to hang his burnished hats,
and our reefs too small for his golden fish.

And as payback, he turned
into a mocking gadfly,
laying his eggs every day
on our wounds.

And now we are nursing wounds

that will not heal.
Our faces twitch with pain
every minute,
the pain
we can no longer hide
from the eyes of anyone.

The Message of Tears

Below my dark brown eyes
many poems have been written
by the tears pouring down my face
every time I open my eyes,
tears that sometimes drift
like an island sliding into the sea,
like migratory birds blinded by the sun,
like a river with too many tributaries.

All over the landscape of my face,
they have carved paths
no one wants to walk,
lines people pretend not to have seen.

And for many recalcitrant seasons,
I was the only one that read their elegies,
the only one who knew the pain
with which every word was written.

I was the only one who bore
the weight of their pain,
the weight that grew heavier each time
I read them silently to myself
so that no one would be offended.

Sometimes they cascaded down my face
as streams with the voices of many seas,
as fountains with the gleaming faces
of lost meteors and stars,
or as rivers flaming with secrets,

secrets that sometimes
drive my unshed tears
into the inner chambers of my sockets,
where like monks,
they quietly bear their sorrows.

But one day, my tears will no longer
be a road no one wants to tread,
a voice no one wants to hear,
or an abhorred trail
gathering dust on my face.
One day, they will write
the poems everyone will read.

Until then, they will continue
to rehearse their dirges on my face,
lamenting of the neglected wounds of Africa—
the message no one wants to hear.

After all, no African
has the right to complain
about the heavy burden of subjugation
and tyranny heaped upon them;

no African has the right to complain
about their thirst or miseries,
or the grueling pain of poverty
wound tightly around their necks
with heavy oppressive chains.
No, not for one day.

Africans are supposed to rejoice
in their moonless nights,
in their sunless dawns,
in the stale air of their prisons,
and for the stipend they earn
with their sweat and blood.

No one cares.
No one really cares,
because Africans are supposed
to live and die in silence.

A Common Poet

You are not alone.
I am also tired of telling
endless stories of woes,
and so is the rain tired of narrating
her woes to deaf ears.
That's why sometimes,
she calls down thunder
to unclog our ears
so that we can hear her
when she pours out her grief.

I also know you are tired
of hearing about Africa's foes.
So am I.

I am tired of drumming them on deaf ears.
So is the wind tired of telling
the repeated stories of her own foes.
And because no one patiently listens
to her melancholic stories,
sometimes, she calls on tornadoes
and hurricanes to strike the deaf
and apathetic earth
with a force that breaks
the bones and hearts of many.

I am not the rain,
I am not the wind.
Just an ordinary poet.
I rehearse words, not wars.
I repeat monodies with fractured alphabets,
not the angry monotones
of the rain
or the wind.

My words are bells,
or drums
to amplify
the secret dreams
in the hearts of Africans.

My letters do not wreck
cities or lives
like tornadoes and hurricanes.
They are the mere words
of an ordinary poet
trying to remind the world
of the unacknowledged
pain
of Africans.

The Sound of Silence

Oh, the sound of silence,
the sound of silence,
how deafening,
how deafening,
in every African city and village.

By day or night,
we speak to each other
only with signs and symbols,
with hands and sealed lips,
with groans and grunts,
and with faces that bare the pain
of every word
swallowed in fear or silence.

The only sound that loosens our tongues
and jolts everyone to their feet
are the footsteps of the slave masters
and their loud puppets.

The echoes of their footsteps
summon us from our squalors
to their throne room where we prostrate
and bow to worship them
until our knees bleed.

And after the long worship and adulations
we huddle in line to receive
the same old instructions
on how to throw our rights,
our names, and dignity
to the dust
and wear our leashes,
our shackles, and marks
of slavery with pride.

But today, I have come
to pry open with my pen
the sealed lips
of our fathers and mothers
until someone speaks and renounces
this life of slavery and misery,
this life between the tyrant's creeds
and the slave master's greed,
that have left us less of human beings—
a people without rights,
or a future.

Today, I have come to remind
every African that it's time to speak,
or we may never recover
from our wounds,
or from the life of slavery.

Nothing will change if we continue

to nurse fear in our shivering
and surrendered hearts.
Nothing will change
until we speak collectively with a voice,
unwilling to surrender any more
our destiny and the destinies of our children
to a perpetual life of subjugation
and exploitation.

Indeed, nothing will change.

The Loud Bells

The daily loud bells of tyranny
and imperialism have dulled
our perception of each other's pain,
making us more distant from each other,
leaving us to bear our burdens alone,
fight our battles alone,
and die alone
in a lonely house.

And if this unmitigated sound
of subjugation continues to rack
our weakened eardrums, our ears
will become irreparably damaged,
leaving us deaf—

deaf to the echoes of our children's heartbeat,
deaf to the scuffing feet of corruption,
deaf to the loud gouges
and cracks in our walls,
deaf to the sound of windows
and doors shut against us.

Now that the moon still stays late
to cheer us up, we must foster
a strong union to tear down

the crushing walls of tyranny;
we must be brave like the moon,
taking bold and fearless strides
in the presence of an angry night.

This loud bell of autocracy
is a cruel and inhuman agony
that we cannot continue to bear.

Brothers and sisters,
elders and kinsmen.
Today, let us rise to silence
this persistent roar
of the tolling bells
before we all become deaf,

and before the sea swells
and reclaims the shores
that we come to each day
to spread our pains like a mat
and lay our wounds bare to heal,

else, we will be remembered
as a generation
whose legacy was nothing
but graveyards and an endless stretch
of a deaf and muted land.

My Pen

It's not a spear.
It's a pen I yell at all day
to flow as fast as one
of the great rivers of Africa.

It's not an arrow.
It's a furrowed pen that sometimes
cannot bear the weight
of many words.

It's not a gravedigger.
It's an engraver that sometimes
cannot endure the rigors
of carving long and tortuous letters.

It's not an idol.
It's a paddle,
a paddle to navigate
the troubled waters of Africa
in search of a safe harbor to dock.

It's not a rivet.
It's a trumpet,
a trumpet that echoes my heartbeat
for the hard hearing ears of the world.

It's not a crosspiece.
It's a mouthpiece,
the mouthpiece of an ordinary poet
bearing the weight
of too many unspoken words.

It's not a hutch.
It's a crutch to prop myself up
when the morning comes
trembling like a leaf
in the landscape of my mind.

With it, I pierce
the veil of darkness
over the face of Africa,
knowing that if we all keep quiet,
we will remain invisible to the world,

and our footprints
will not be recognized
or acknowledged,
no matter how deep
we engrave them on the ground.

Corollaries

After many years of silence,
the putrid pods hidden
by the leaves of our culpable trees
fractured their lips,
spitting their offal in our faces.
Now, our land has been engulfed
by the nauseating smell of putrefaction.

It seemed when the sky became tired
of seeing evil, it heaved in anger,
violently shaking its vault
until it discharged into the atmosphere
all the filth it inherited from our land.

The air is thick with death.
Everywhere you look,
the flurries of battered years
are seen falling
like a cursed rain,
like a sea of dust,
like a hideous night.

Our sins have confronted us.
Our hands and feet have been stained
by our own filth,

and all around us
an unsettling gloom stares
from a subdued landscape.

Everyone is afraid,
afraid of this unrelenting hand of evil,
except for our leaders—
lords and gods
with opulent bubbles
nothing has ever darkened.

Today, my pen finds no resting place
between my fingers,
not with the threats from every side—
threats from the weakening levees
keeping away the surrounding seas,
threats from the angry sky,
and threats from the day
that has become a devouring night.

Ikechi Akurunwa

FOUR

There is only one destination for Africa—
FREEDOM!
There is no going back.

The Last African Frontier

Oh, African child,
son of the embattled continent.
Don't forget that before those mocking
effigies of captivity and death
were wound around our necks
with the twisted thread of history,
there were fulfilled and free Africans
pursuing their dreams.

Don't forget that the old fingerprints
and footprints of Africa's greatness
were erased
by the trampling feet of colonialism
to desecrate the revered thrones
of African kings.

Before the roots of our trees rotted,
our ground was already poisoned
by greedy treasure hunters from Europe
digging for the last vestige
of Africa's gold and oil.

So, don't wait for the mourning moon
to shed all her tears weeping for Africa
before you begin to rip off

the cuffs of imperialism
from the hands and feet of Africa,
else the moon's bloody tears
will mask the spilled blood
of fallen Africans,
hiding the tracks of evil.

And don't wait for the angry day
to open more of its hidden doors
to vicious predators
waiting to invade Africa
from all over the world,
before you build a hedge
around Africa's vulnerable shores.

Don't wait, oh African child;
don't wait for one more day.
Death is still charging through our streets
like an enraged bull.
And poverty, the old bully,
is still ravaging our land,
daily tormenting
dead
and living Africans.

Nothing has changed
and nothing will change
if you don't rise to reclaim Africa.

You and your generation
are Africa's last frontier.

In the End

Don't be fooled by the gleaming
face of the calm sea.
Wait until it goes into an epileptic fit
and you will see how ugly it can be.

Don't be fooled by the wave's gentle gestures
when it nibbles your feet.
Wait until its neck is twisted by torticollis
to see what torment it endures.

Don't be fooled by the bluster
of a roaring lion.
Wait until mange grows on its head
to see how pathetic the lion can be.

Don't be discouraged by a tyrant's rant.
Wait until a debilitating sickness visits him,
and his hands and feet
will grow limp.

In the end, life has a way
of humbling or taming us,
and if all fails, it can use
the iron hands of death to silence us, forever.

Nighthawks

The night has a well-kept secret
that the prying eyes
of the moon and the stars
have not been able to unravel.

That is why I wonder
where those who plough
through the night with closed eyes
are heading.

The heart that does not know
the difference between
night and day, or right and wrong,
has crossed the line between life and death,
between sanity and insanity.

It is the heart of a soul
that wears the night as a mask,
nighthawk that hides in darkness,
forgetting that no matter
how long the night lingers,
morning will surely come.

Sticks or Legs

Each stride bears a message,
a message of silence or credence,
a message of fear or courage.

Every bold stride is a bell
rung resoundingly to the deaf world,
a sword drawn against an obstacle
by those who don't carry their legs
like brittle sticks.

When your footsteps sound like thunder,
the ground will shake,
shifting somethings back
to their rightful places,
and dislodging somethings
forced into the wrong places.

Even the sleeping world is woken up
and forced to look in your direction.

But when your footsteps
cannot cause
even a fly to bat an eye,
things will remain the way they are,
or grow worse.

Friend, in your feet, lies
the power to trample
on hills and mountains
until they become plains,

the power to plow through wild woods,
brick walls, or frozen rivers,
until you turn them into thoroughfares;

the power to pound your footprints
on the rugged and stubborn earth
until they become indelible,

and the power to kick
the dividing walls
of racism, poverty, and injustice,
day and night,
until they crumble.

But if you are not willing to endure
a few lacerations and bruises,
and sometimes broken bones,

your leg will remain nothing
but walking sticks
bearing the weight
of an inconsequential soul.

The Story of the Black Man

How long has the West insisted
that the world does not need
the black man?

How long have they sought
ways to subvert him and possibly
banish him, permanently,
from the face of the earth?

It's their secret desire,
their consuming obsession,
the thought daily occupying
their proud and vain hearts.

And if today, they see a black man
trying to plant a flag on Mars,
they will quickly dismiss it
as the sighting of a ghost,
or explain it away,
like any of their other
fairy tales about Africa.

Yet, everywhere you go
around the world
you will see an African

or someone with an African root,
upon whose shoulder
the world has confidently
rested part of its weight.

And whether appreciated or not;
accorded any respect or not,
properly rewarded or not,
he remains undaunted,
undeterred and unstoppable.

Colonial Masters

So, half of Africa is Africa's
and the other half is the invader's colony
with their armories and military bases
strategically planted in our farms and yards
like a forest of thorns that no one can tread on.

And because of this insidious occupation—
only half of Africa is free,
the other half is in chains;
only one eye of Africa can see,
the other is blind;
only one ear of Africa can hear,
the other is deaf;
only one leg of Africa is useful,
the other is lame.

Every day, the colonial master's
lethal weapons of perpetual imperialism
slowly transforms Africa
into a continent inhabited
by people that are either
half dead or half alive.

But all hope is not lost.
One day, Africa will undoubtedly be free

because freedom is a human right,
the right no one can indefinitely
deny a people determined to be free.

Beyond Their Power

Every night,
I admire how the stars
brazenly burn
in the angry African night.

There is no doubt
that those who vainly parade themselves
in superfluous robes and crowns
will never burn brighter than any of the stars,
no matter how hard they try.

And there is no ambiguity of fact
that those arrogating themselves
as the gods of Africa or the earth
will not be able to extinguish
the flames of all the stars,
no matter how long they swing their hands
and magic wands
in the air.

That is why every night,
I do not waste my time
counting the stars
shining bright over my roof,
because I know they will be there

all night with the moon
to guide the feet of every pilgrim
to the dawn of a new day.

Not Forever

How loud can the angry lion roar?
How far can the fiery bullet travel?
How thin can the cruel thorn sharpen its teeth?
If you ask me, I will say,
only for a little while,
only for a little while.

How long can the harsh winter tarry?
How hard can the stubborn rock harden?
How deep can the root of a greedy weed dig?
If you ask me, I will say,
not indefinitely,
not indefinitely.

How long can the night linger?
How long can it linger in the streets,
in the hallways, in the corridors?
How long can it hover
over the sea like a dark cloud,
or hang itself on walls
like the haunting shadow of a ghost?

How long can it hide
its mournful face in the attic,
in empty shells or nests,

or behind fences and walls,
like the shadow of death?

How long can it hold onto
the brittle boughs of darkness,
or jump from roof to roof,
or swing from hammock to hammock,

or dock underneath bridges and in bushes
as fireflies, glow worms, the moon,
and stars with flickering flashlights,
try to chase it away?

If you ask me, I will say,
not for too long,
because I know that soon
it will be morning,
and darkness will have nowhere to hide.

Oh Sweet Land of Africa

Long before I saw your face
you saw my face forming
in the invisible mirror of your mind.

And while I grew in your womb,
each journey
that left scars on your face,
you went with me.

Each time you fought for a place
to firmly plant the sole of your feet,
you were fighting
for my future,
for my dreams,
for a place that I will one day
water until roses unfold,
inviting the birds and the bees
to a choral debate of varying
tones and notations.

In each of your footprints
you watched with delight
my tiny footprint forming
like a shadow slowly
asserting its presence,

like rays of the sun
marking the niche
of a new blade,

like a minuscule grain of corn
growing confidently
in the middle of a vast cornfield.

Though in your journeys
you have been whiplashed, sunstruck,
and drenched with rain,
but nothing has been able
to dampen your spirit—
nothing!

And each day, as you filled
the air of the African dawn
with your songs of hope,
carnations emerged from their shadows.
Each day you breathed hope
into the dying nostrils of the poor
with your sweet melodies,
each leaf of each tree,
and each mouth of each bird
sang with you.

And until you held me in your loving arms
your delightful serenades
made the harsh voice of the world

barely audible.

Sweet land of Africa,
oh, sweet land of Africa,
now that I have seen your face,
how I love you even more,
how I love your garment
adorned with tribal marks,
how I love your multilingual tongues
that no continent can boast of,
how I love your great rivers and seas,
your great mountains and valleys,
your incredible waterfalls and fountains.
All this has made you
the envy of the world.

Great and fragrant land of Africa,
the land of my birth,
the land my forefathers have fought for ages
to take back from the hands of Europe,
now that we have each other by our sides
our burdens have become lighter,

and together we will keep
the African dream
forever alive in our hearts.

The Great Task

Son, in Africa, there are still leaves yet to grow
and fruits yet to ripen on our trees.
There are still birds with songs no one has heard.
There are still stones sitting
on acres of gold and diamonds
no one has uncovered.

So, son, Africa is still a land to conquer,
a land of beautiful verses,
and beautiful carnations,
and gorgeous hills and mountains
waiting for you to conquer.

But for you to conquer the land of Africa,
you must muscle your way
through the old steel walls of colonialism,
and scale over the high mountains of tyranny,
and scheme safely through lands
full of landmines planted
to keep you imprisoned in fear.

It is only after you have accomplished these feats
that Africa will become yours,
and all that has made Africa
grimace in pain day and night

will cease.

And all the stain on her face
from her head being constantly
drowned in the filth of poverty,
will be erased.
Her legs caught in the claws
of subjugation and meaningless wars,
will be freed.

Son, it will not be easy.
But if you do nothing,
you will never be free,
and your children will never be free.

If you do nothing,
you will live and die without dignity,
and without seeing
Africa's leaves and fruits
that are yet to bud and bloom.

If you do nothing,
the night will continue to linger,
and morning will never come.

The Time

Every day our lives touch so many things,
and are touched by so many things,
but unlike the dust,
we don't surrender
or give up our place in life
without a fight.

The dusts are blown from coast to coast,
hauled by the wind
and by every moving object
until they become part
of another earth crust,
or lost somewhere
in the inscrutable universe.

Africa is not a load of dust.
She is a soul, a beautiful soul,
a soul groaning for freedom,
a soul yawning for a new dawn.

Today, let us pledge
to never give up our place,
to never give up our rights,
to never give up our dreams,
without a fight.

This is the time
for all enraged African seas,
all inflamed stars and moon in the African sky,
and all fed-up sons and daughters of Africa
to rise
to firmly establish
that we are in charge
of our destiny,
and not the West,
or the world.

Journey

All through this journey with you
I pierced the dark veil
over the face of Africa,
stirring the venom
in the mouth of the night
with the tip of my pen.

I peered into the abyss
with flames from my iris
each time I scrubbed the stain
of poverty on the skin of Africa
with the rivers of my tears.

With a broken voice,
I screamed in the ears
of those who made less of her pain,
waving her tatters in the air
for every eye to see what was left
of Africa's great fortunes.

The days were long and arduous,
nights lingered forever,
but I journeyed on,
amidst sunburns and rainstorms,
knowing that Africa

is the root I am proud to have,
the crown I am proud to wear,
and the canvas I am proud to fill
with the paintings of my dream.

Many times, I laid my tired head
upon her shoulders
and held her hands as we wept
until the tears dripping from her eyes
began to seep from my pen.

She sang for me each time
joy began to fade from my face.
She sang for me until the lyrics
that issued from her wounded heart
became the song I sang all day
as we journeyed together,
along scalding and rugged paths,
towards the coming dawn.

Hold the Fort

Dear African patriots,
remember you are the ones
left to fly the flag of freedom,
the ones left to kick the walls
of subjugation and imprisonment
until they fall.

Therefore, hold the fort.
Don't back down.
There is no land the determined sea
cannot recover,
no darkness the sun cannot erase.

No matter how dark the night grows
or how loud it growls,
hold the fort,
hold the fort,
don't back down.

One day, we will smile again,
we will laugh again,
we will dream again.
One day, we will be again
a free and happy people,
in the land of Africa.

Until blood begins to flow again
in the veins of my exhausted pen,
until time and fate
give us our next assignment,
hold the fort,
hold the fort,
don't back down,

for morning
will surely come.

www.ingramcontent.com/pod-product-compliance
Lightning Source LLC
Chambersburg PA
CBHW031559040426
42452CB00006B/355